KID SCIENCE

KITCHEN SCIENCE EXPERIMENTS

Q. L. Pearce

ROXBURY PARK

LOWELL HOUSE JUVENILE

LOS ANGELES

NTC/Contemporary Publishing Group

With love to Kaitlyn,
the best kitchen helper I could ask for
—Q. P.

Published by Lowell House
A division of NTC/Contemporary Publishing Group, Inc.
4255 West Touhy Avenue, Lincolnwood (Chicago), Illinois 60646-1975 U.S.A.

Lowell House books can be purchased at special discounts when ordered in bulk for premiums and special sales. Contact Department CS at the following address:

NTC/Contemporary Publishing Group
4255 West Touhy Avenue
Lincolnwood, IL 60646-1975
1-800-323-4900

ISBN: 0-7373-0285-2
Library of Congress Catalog Card Number: 99-74665

Roxbury Park is a division of NTC/Contemporary Publishing Group, Inc.

Managing Director and Publisher: Jack Artenstein
Editor in Chief, Roxbury Park Books: Michael Artenstein
Director of Publishing Services: Rena Copperman
Editorial Assistant: Nicole Monastirsky
Freelance Editor: Sara Gooch
Interior Artist: Sophie Sheppard
Interior Designer: Carolyn Wendt

Printed and bound in the United States of America
00 01 RDD 10 9 8 7 6 5 4 3 2

Date Due Receipt

02/21/2017

Items checked out to

Stenzinger, Ally

TITLE How to write codes and send
BARCODE   30613000368450
DUE   03-14-17 00:00AM
TITLE Kitchen science experiments
BARCODE   30613001180201
DUE   03-14-17 00:00AM

Date Due Receipt

Items checked out to

TITLE How to write codes and send
DUE 03-14-17 00:00AM

TITLE Kitchen science experiments
BARCODE 30813001180201
DUE 03-14-17 00:00AM

CONTENTS

GETTING STARTED WITH KITCHEN SCIENCE

How does a straw work? What happens when you mix baking soda and vinegar? How much sugar can you stir into a full glass of water? The answers to these questions and more are as near as your own kitchen. With a few simple materials, you can test the chemical composition of a potato, remove the shell from a raw egg without touching it, and turn milk into plastic.

Here are some basic safety tips:

- Before you begin, read the directions completely.

- Wear old clothing or an apron.

- Never put an unknown material into your mouth or near your eyes.

- Label any long-term experiments that will be kept in your refrigerator or freezer.

- Use padded gloves when working with hot water.

- Clean up your work area.

- Wash your hands when you are finished.

You may need an adult helper for some of the experiments in this book. Most of the materials you'll need for these experiments are probably already in your home. Check with an adult before you use any household supplies.

Are you ready for some fun? Then let's go to the kitchen and get started.

THE DISAPPEARING SHELL

It may seem impossible to peel a raw egg, but it can be done. This experiment will show you how to use a "chemical peel."

Setup time: 5 minutes ● **Observation time:** 3 days

MATERIALS

raw egg   glass quart jar with lid   vinegar

DIRECTIONS

2 hours

1. Carefully place the egg into the glass jar.

2. Fill the jar three-fourths full with vinegar.

3. Observe the egg after 2 hours. Are bubbles forming?

4. Leave the jar undisturbed for 3 days, checking occasionally.

3 days

5. After 3 days, remove the lid, place your hand over the jar opening, and slowly pour the vinegar into a sink. Carefully allow the egg to slip into your hand. Handle it very gently as you observe it because it will break easily. How is the egg different? What is missing?

ACTION, REACTION, RESULTS

By the end of this experiment, the shell of the egg is dissolved due to a chemical reaction between the shell and the vinegar. The shell is made of calcium carbonate that breaks down and creates carbon dioxide gas when exposed to vinegar, a mild acid. You see the bubbles of gas forming on the eggshell. The bubbling continues until the eggshell is completely used up.

WORD FILE

Chemical reaction: A chemical change that occurs when two or more substances interact with each other.

Dissolve: To make a solid or gas disappear into a liquid.

BLOW UP

Here's a way to blow up a balloon without wasting a single breath.

Setup time: 15 minutes • **Observation time:** 5 minutes

MATERIALS

 plastic 12-ounce soda bottle

 petroleum jelly

tissue paper

 1 tablespoon baking soda

 ½ cup vinegar

balloon with a neck large enough to slip tightly over the opening of the soda bottle

DIRECTIONS

1. Lightly coat the rim of the soda bottle with petroleum jelly.

2. Tear a square of tissue about 2 inches square. Place a tablespoon of baking soda onto the tissue. Roll the tissue into a tube around the baking soda and twist the ends closed.

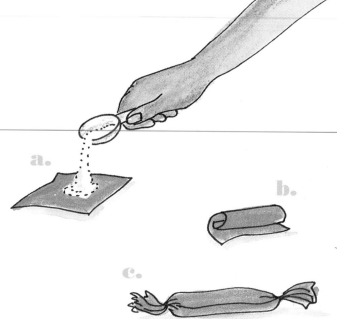

a.

b.

c.

Gas Expansion

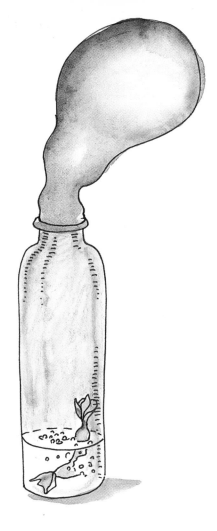

3. Pour the vinegar into the soda bottle. Drop the baking soda packet into the bottle.

4. Moving quickly, slip the neck of the balloon over the opening of the bottle and hold it in place. What happens?

ACTION, REACTION, RESULTS

When the tissue paper tears and the baking soda and vinegar meet, a chemical reaction takes place. Carbon dioxide, a gas, is produced. The gas expands out of the bottle and into the balloon, blowing it up.

GOING, GOING, GONE

Mix a cup of sugar into a cup of water and you'll have two cups of fluid. Right? Maybe not.

Setup time: 20 minutes • **Observation time:** 20 minutes

MATERIALS

 glass quart jar   2 measuring cups   water

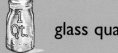 marker   spoon   sugar

DIRECTIONS

1. Prepare the jar by filling it with 1 cup of water. Mark the water level with the marker. Pour in a second cup of water and mark the level. Empty the jar.

2. Pour 1 cup of water into the jar. It should come to the level of the first mark.

3. Pour 1 cup of sugar into the jar and stir. Does the solution reach the level of the second mark? Where did the sugar go?

You can't see it, but there is plenty of space in the jar of water. The space is in between the water molecules. As you stir in the sugar, it dissolves and the sugar molecules slip into the spaces between the water molecules. Because of this, a cup of sugar stirred into a cup of water will measure less than two cups.

WORD FILE

Molecule: The smallest particle of a substance that can exist alone and have all the characteristics of that substance.

Solution: The result of combining a solute—in this case, sugar—with a solvent—in this case, water.

EYE TO EYE

It's fun to plant a seed and watch it sprout and grow. Here's a way to enjoy a newly sprouting plant without planting a seed.

Setup time: 30 minutes ● **Observation time:** 2 weeks

MATERIALS

 potato knife

 small clay pot with saucer potting soil water

DIRECTIONS

1. Look for an "eye" on the potato. It is a small, round spot that is slightly rough to the touch.

2. Ask an adult helper to cut a 1-inch square from the potato that includes an eye.

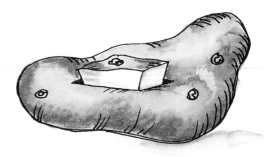

WORD FILE

Root: A plant part that grows down into the soil and doesn't have leaves or buds. It anchors the plant in place and absorbs water and minerals from the soil.

Seed: A small, self-contained body, produced by a flowering plant, that can sprout under proper conditions.

Stem: The part of a plant that bears leaves and stems.

2 weeks

3. Fill the clay pot with potting soil. Plant the square of potato 1 inch deep with the eye at the top. Cover it loosely with soil. Put the pot on a saucer. Water the soil until it is damp but not soaking.

4. Place the pot and saucer in a warm, sunny spot. Over the next 2 weeks, keep the soil moist and watch for your new plant to sprout.

ACTiON, REACTiON, RESULTS

You don't always need seeds to grow a new plant. Many plants can grow from some part of a parent plant, such as a leaf, stem, or root. This is called vegetative propagation. A potato is a tuber, the swollen end of an underground stem. There are tiny buds and scale leaves on the tuber that can each sprout into a new plant. The potato itself is the food source for the sprout as it grows.

Potatoes can also be grown from seeds. Some farmers prefer to use the eyes of the potato, called sets, because the result is more predictable than with a seed-grown crop.

READY, SET, BOIL

You've probably heard the old saying, "A watched pot never boils."
What about a salted pot?

Setup time: 10 minutes • **Observation time:** 15 minutes

MATERIALS

 2 small pots

 cold water

 3 tablespoons salt

 spoon

 stove

DIRECTIONS

1. Fill each pot halfway with water.

2. Add 3 tablespoons of salt to the first pot.

3. Place each pot on a burner on the stove. Ask an adult to supervise as you turn each burner on high.

4. Wait for the water to boil. Which pot starts to boil first?

5. Note the time that the first pot boils. How much longer does it take before the second pot boils?

ACTION, REACTION, RESULTS

WORD FILE

Boiling point: The point at which something changes from a liquid to a gas or vapor.

Molecule: The smallest unit of a material that still has the characteristics of that material.

The unsalted water reaches its boiling point first. The salt molecules in the salty water have a higher boiling point than water, so they interfere with the process. It takes longer because the salted water must reach a higher temperature before it will boil.

Salting the water when you are cooking can speed up your cooking time because the water boils at a higher temperature.

RISING ICE

Most substances contract when they freeze, but not water.

Setup time: 20 minutes ● **Observation time:** 4 hours

MATERIALS

  pint jar clay 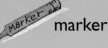 plastic straw

measuring cup water 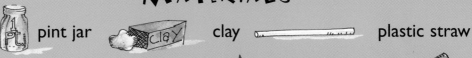 food coloring marker

DIRECTIONS

1. Press a walnut-sized ball of clay inside the jar at the center of the bottom.

2. Stick the straw firmly into the clay so that it stands straight up.

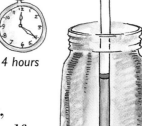

4 hours

3. Mix a few drops of food coloring into ½ cup of water, then slowly pour the water into the straw until it is half filled. Don't worry if some spills. Mark the water level on the straw with a marker. Place the jar in the freezer.

4. After 4 hours the water will be frozen. Check the level of the ice in the straw. Is it higher?

ACTION, REACTION, RESULTS

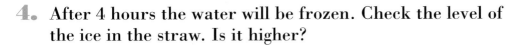

Water has some unusual properties. Unlike most substances, water expands when it reaches its freezing point. When frozen, the water molecules join together in a hexagonal structure that takes up more space than water molecules do in liquid form.

WORD FILE

Freezing point: The point at which a liquid becomes a solid.

Hexagonal: Having a six-sided shape.

SPARKLE AND SHINE

Certain substances are made of crystals, glasslike solids with regular shapes. With this experiment, you can have fun while creating your own crop of crystals.

Setup time: 15 minutes ● **Observation time:** 3 days

MATERIALS

 teacup scissors

 black construction paper measuring cup

 salt  water spoon

DIRECTIONS

1. Cut a shape (such as a flower, an animal, or a star) from the black construction paper. Be sure it fits and will stand up in the teacup. Place the construction paper cutout inside the cup in an upright position.

2. Mix salt into ½ cup of water. Keep adding salt until no more will dissolve.

3. Fill the teacup with about ½ inch of salty water. Keep the cutout standing up. Set the cup in a warm, dry place. Let it remain undisturbed for 3 days or until all the water has evaporated. What has been left behind on the construction paper?

3 days

ACTION, REACTION, RESULTS

The salty water moves up through the construction paper by capillary action. Tiny fibers that make up the paper have spaces between them. Water molecules move through the spaces by adhering to the fibers. As the water molecules move up, they attract and draw up water molecules from below. As the water in the construction paper dries, it leaves behind deposits of salt crystals, particularly along the upper edge of the paper.

MOLECULES ON THE MOVE

Take a close look at a glass of water. Can you see the water moving? You can't always believe your eyes because even though the water looks still, it is in motion.

Setup time: 5 minutes ● **Observation time:** 20 minutes

MATERIALS

 pint jar   water    food coloring

DIRECTIONS

1. Fill the pint jar to the top with cool tap water. Place the jar on a flat surface where it will not be disturbed.

2. Tap several drops of food coloring into the water. Don't stir it. What does the food coloring do?

3. Check the jar after 20 minutes. How does the food coloring look now?

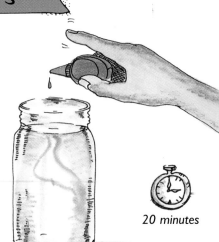

20 minutes

ACTION, REACTION, RESULTS

WORD FILE

Diffusion: The spreading of molecules of a substance through another substance.

Particle: A tiny part of a substance, such as a grain of sand or a molecule.

The water molecules in the jar are always on the move. They are so tiny that you can't see them move, but you can see the effect they have on the food coloring. As the streams of color settle, the particles of food coloring are hit by water molecules sending them in all different directions. Within an hour the color is evenly spread just by the moving molecules.

MAKING MUSIC

How would you like to put on a little concert in your kitchen?
Here's a way to make and play your own musical instrument.

Setup time: 20 minutes ● **Observation time:** As long as you want!

MATERIALS

 six 12-ounce glass soda bottles water spoon

DIRECTIONS

1. Line up the soda bottles on a flat surface with 2 inches of space between them.

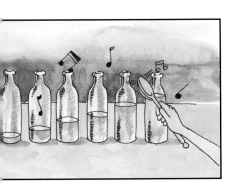

2. Fill the first bottle with about ½ inch of water. Fill the next bottle ½ inch higher than the first. Continue to fill each bottle ½ inch higher than the bottle before it.

3. Holding the spoon loosely, tap each bottle near the top. Is there a difference in the sound that each bottle makes? Just for fun, try to tap out a tune.

ACTION, REACTION, RESULTS

Sound is actually waves of vibrations. When you tap the bottles with the spoon you cause them to vibrate. The vibrations travel in waves through the air into your ear. You perceive the vibrations as sound. The number of vibrations is called the frequency of the sound. The bottle with the least amount of water vibrates the most and has the highest pitch. The bottle with the most water vibrates the least and has the lowest pitch.

WORD FILE

Pitch: A characteristic of sound; a measure of the frequency of a vibration. A high frequency vibration produces a note of high pitch.

Vibration: To move regularly backward and forward.

HEART THROB

If you like marshmallows, you'll see more than you bargained for with this experiment.

Setup time: 15 minutes • **Observation time:** 5 minutes

MATERIALS

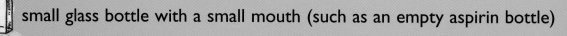 small glass bottle with a small mouth (such as an empty aspirin bottle)

 miniature marshmallow — sharp-pointed marker

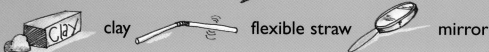 clay — flexible straw — mirror

DIRECTIONS

1. Draw a heart on the marshmallow and put it into the bottle. Place the marshmallow so that the heart is facing outward.

2. Put about an inch of the straw into the bottle, then seal the opening of the bottle closed with clay. Use enough clay to seal it completely and hold the straw in place.

3. Set up a mirror on a table so that you can watch the marshmallow as you perform the experiment.

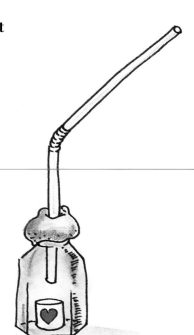

18

4. Suck the air out of the bottle through the straw. Keep the straw in your mouth as you look in the mirror. What happens to the marshmallow?

5. Release the straw to allow the air back into the bottle. Now what happens to the marshmallow?

Action, Reaction, Results

There is air all around everything, and it pushes in all directions. There is air in the bottle and in the marshmallow. When you suck out the air through the straw you lower the air pressure in the bottle. The air that is left expands to take up the available space. The air-filled marshmallow expands, too. As you watch in the mirror you can see the heart get bigger. When you allow the air back into the bottle, the marshmallow returns to its original size.

> **WORD FILE**
>
> **Air pressure:** The pushing or squeezing force that air exerts on everything it touches.

SKIN TIGHT

Water has a stretchy skin. In this experiment, you will demonstrate a property of that unusual skin.

Setup time: 15 minutes ● **Observation time:** 5 minutes

MATERIALS

 bowl at least 8 inches across

 water

 7 wooden toothpicks

 dishwashing soap

DIRECTIONS

1. Set the bowl on a flat surface and fill it with water. Wait for the water to stop moving.

2. Carefully arrange six toothpicks on the surface of the water with their tips pointing toward the center in a "sunburst" pattern. Use the other toothpick to move them around.

3. Squirt a drop of dishwashing soap into the water at the center of the bowl. What happens?

ACTION, REACTION, RESULTS

Molecules near the surface of the water have a tendency to "cling" to each other creating a stretchy "skin" called surface tension. The toothpicks float on the skin. Putting the drop of soap in the center weakens the cling at that point. The skin is drawn to the edges of the bowl, and the toothpicks are drawn along with it.

> The water strider is an insect that spends most of its time on water. This lightweight creature doesn't sink because it is supported by surface tension.

MARVELOUS MIST

Plants often enjoy a spritz of water. Here's a way to make a simple mist sprayer that your plants will appreciate.

Setup time: 5 minutes • **Observation time:** 5 minutes

MATERIALS

drinking glass   plant   water

2 plastic straws   scissors

DIRECTIONS

1. Set the glass next to the plant on a flat surface.

2. Fill the glass with water.

3. Trim one straw so that it is 1 inch higher than the rim of the glass.

4. Facing the plant, hold the second straw at a right angle to the first straw. Blow gently through the second straw, and you will see the water level rise in the first.

5. Blow very hard through the second straw. What happens?

ACTION, REACTION, RESULTS

Air pressure pushes down on the water in the glass, pushing water up into the straw. As you blow into the second straw and across the first, you lower the air pressure over the first straw causing the water in it to rise. Once the water reaches the top of the straw, tiny droplets are carried by the gust of air you are blowing. The droplets reach the plant as a fine, cool mist.

Perfume often comes in a special bottle called an atomizer. The atomizer works much like the plant sprayer you made. It has a large, flexible bulb that creates airflow when it is squeezed, and that airflow helps to deliver a fine mist of perfume.

FRUIT POWER

If your flashlight batteries go dim, you may be able to find a replacement in the fruit drawer of your refrigerator.

Setup time: 30 minutes • **Observation time:** 5 minutes

MATERIALS

 lemon brass thumbtack

 steel paper clip two 3-inch pieces of electrical wire

 low-voltage flashlight bulb small knife

DIRECTIONS

1. Ask an adult to strip 1½ inches of insulation from both ends of each piece of electrical wire with the small knife.

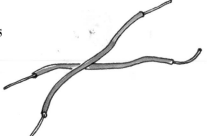

2. Take one piece of wire and wrap one end around the brass tack and the other end around the base of the flashlight bulb. Take the second piece of wire and wrap one end around the paper clip and the other end around the base of the flashlight bulb.

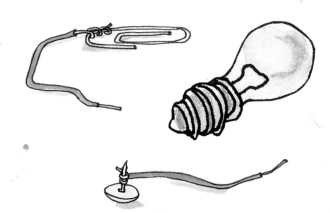

3. Insert both the brass tack and the paper clip into lemon, as shown. What happens?

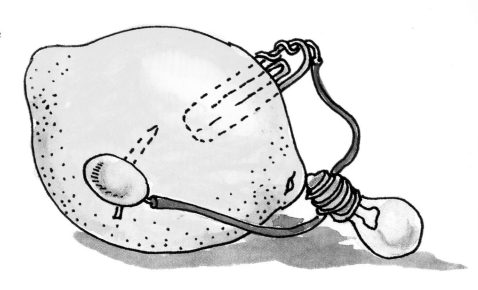

ACTION, REACTION, RESULTS

Electricity is generated when materials combine and create chemical reactions. A battery is a portable method of providing electricity. In a battery, there is a chemical called an electrolyte between two metal electrodes. In this demonstration, the acid in the lemon acts as the electrolyte and reacts with the metal in the tack and paper clip which act as electrodes. When the lemon, electrical wire, and bulb are connected, they create an electrical circuit that makes the bulb light up.

Batteries are used in many ways. Look around your own home and count any items that may be battery powered. Don't forget radios, clocks, and toys. How many can you find?

GOOEY MOO

That milk in your refrigerator can take a totally different and fun form.

Setup time: 15 minutes ● **Observation time:** 5 minutes

MATERIALS

 1 cup whole milk   saucepan

 ½ cup vinegar   stove

DIRECTIONS

1. Pour the milk into a saucepan. Ask an adult to help you warm the milk to a slow boil.

2. Add the vinegar and stir slowly until the mixture becomes rubbery.

 WORD FILE

Carbon: An element. Carbon compounds are found in many plants and animals.

3. Let the material cool, then rinse it under cool running water. What does it remind you of? What can you do with it?

ACTION, REACTION, RESULTS

Milk contains a substance called carbon, which reacts with the acid in the vinegar. The result is a plasticlike substance that can be molded into shapes and even bounced.

CATCH YOUR BREATH

With two straws in your mouth and one in a glass of water, can you still drink?

Setup time: 5 minutes • **Observation time:** 5 minutes

MATERIALS

 drinking glass water 2 straws

DIRECTIONS

1. Place the glass on a flat surface and fill it to the rim with water.

2. Place both straws in your mouth.

3. Put one straw into the water-filled glass and let the other straw remain outside the glass.

4. Try to draw in a drink of water through the straw that is in the glass.

ACTION, REACTION, RESULTS

WORD FILE

Vacuum: A space that is completely empty with no molecules of any kind in it.

When you drink through a straw, you lower the pressure in your mouth and create a partial vacuum. The outside air pressure pushes down on the fluid in the glass and forces it up the straw. By sucking through two straws (one in the liquid and one in the air), you can't form a partial vacuum. The straw in the air creates a leak. The air pressure in your mouth remains the same as that outside, and no liquid is forced up the straw. The fluid remains in the glass.

STARCH DETECTIVE

Starch, as a carbohydrate, can be an important part of the human diet. In this experiment, you can make starch show up in a common food.

Setup time: 20 minutes • **Observation time:** 5 minutes

MATERIALS

 peeled potato   grater   strainer

 paper towel   salt 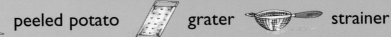 tincture of iodine

DIRECTIONS

1. Grate a tablespoon of potato into a strainer.

2. Press the potato through the strainer onto a paper towel to make a small pile of mushy potato. Place ¼ teaspoon of salt on the paper towel near the potato.

3. Place 2 drops of tincture of iodine on the salt, then 2 drops on the potato. What do you see?

ACTION, REACTION, RESULTS

Due to a chemical reaction, iodine turns blue-black in the presence of starch. The drop of iodine on the salt does not change color because there is no starch in the salt. The drop of iodine on the potato turns blue-black. Starch is a carbohydrate that is converted by the body to simple sugars and used as fuel.

WORD FILE

Carbohydrate: A compound made up of carbon, hydrogen, and oxygen.

Plants store some of the food they make during photosynthesis as starch. The starch may be stored in seeds and stems or roots and underground stems, as in the case of the potato. Foods containing starch can help fuel your energy.

THE NOSE KNOWS

A bad cold can ruin your appetite. That's partly because when your nose is stuffed up, you can't smell your food. Your nose is your mouth's partner when it's time to taste.

Setup time: 15 minutes • **Observation time:** 5 minutes

MATERIALS

 peeled apple peeled raw potato grater

 2 identical small bowls stick-on labels marker

DIRECTIONS

1. Grate a small amount of apple and put it into a bowl. Grate a small amount of potato and put it into the second bowl. Label each bowl on the bottom so that you can only see it by lifting the bowl.

WORD FILE

Pharynx: A cavity at the back of the mouth where the oral and nasal cavities meet.

Tastebuds: Tiny bodies that contain receptors that gather and send taste information to the brain.

2. Close your eyes and mix up the bowls so that you can't tell which is which.

3. Hold your nose and taste the food from each bowl. Can you taste which is which?

4. Taste each food without holding your nose. Is it easier to taste the difference?

Action, Reaction, Results

The sense of smell and sense of taste work together. The nose and mouth share the same airway—the pharynx. The tastebuds on the tongue and palate can determine whether something is sweet, salty, bitter, or sour. The odor of a food helps you to distinguish more subtle flavors.

BRRRRR

Can anything be colder than ice?
Check out this experiment and decide for yourself.

Setup time: 10 minutes • **Observation time:** 2 minutes

MATERIALS

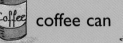 coffee can crushed ice water

outdoor thermometer salt spoon

DIRECTIONS

1. Fill the coffee can halfway with crushed ice. Add water to cover the ice.

2. Place the thermometer in the can. Wait 1 minute, then read the temperature.

1 minute

WORD FILE

Freezing point:
The point at which a liquid becomes a solid.

3. Stir in 2 teaspoons of salt. Wait 1 minute, then read the temperature again. Did it change?

I minute

ACTION, REACTION, RESULTS

Plain, unsalted water freezes at 32 degrees Fahrenheit. Salt lowers the freezing point of water. In this experiment, heat energy from the water is used up as the salt dissolves. As heat is removed from the water, the temperature drops. Salt water freezes at about 28.6 degrees Fahrenheit.

BUBBLE UP

Do you like sugar? A common fungus also uses sugar as food. Most plants make their own food. This experiment will help you learn about those that don't.

Setup time: 15 minutes ● **Observation time:** 24 hours

MATERIALS

 1 package powdered yeast    1 tablespoon sugar

 measuring cup   12-ounce glass soda bottle

 warm water   balloon (with neck large enough to fit tightly over the bottle opening)

DIRECTIONS

1. Mix the yeast and sugar into 1 cup of comfortably warm water. Pour the fluid into the glass bottle.

2. Slip the neck of the balloon over the opening of the bottle.

3. Place the bottle in a dark, warm place where it will not be disturbed. Check the bottle after 1 hour. What has happened?

I hour

4. Check the bottle again after 12 hours. What has happened? Check one final time after 24 hours.

12 hours

24 hours

ACTION, REACTION, RESULTS

Green plants use chlorophyll in their food-making process. Some plants called fungi do not have chlorophyll. Yeast is a fungus. It uses food, such as sugar, as fuel. During the process, carbon dioxide gas is produced. The bubbles you see in the bottle during the experiment are carbon dioxide gas. The gas expands and fills the balloon.

WORD FILE

Chlorophyll: A green substance in plants used to convert sunlight, air, and water into food.

Expands: To get larger in size or volume.

Fungi: Plural of fungus.

Fungus: A single-celled or threadlike plant that contains no chlorophyll.

Some fungi cause disease and can be dangerous. Others are helpful. Certain fungi feed on dead organisms and help to get rid of them. Yeast is a fungus used to bake bread. It feeds on the sugar in the dough and produces carbon dioxide gas that causes the bread to rise.

DROP BY DROP

Surprise your friends with this remarkable demonstration of attraction.

Setup time: 10 minutes ● **Observation time:** 5 minutes

MATERIALS

 waxed paper cup of water

straw toothpick

DIRECTIONS

1. Place a sheet of waxed paper on a flat surface.

2. Dip one end of the straw into the cup of water. Place your thumb over the open end of the straw and lift it out of the water. A droplet will be trapped in the straw.

WORD FILE

Cohesion: Attractive force between molecules of the same type.

Molecule: The smallest unit of a material that still has the characteristics of that material.

3. Lift your thumb to release the trapped droplet onto the waxed paper. Make three more drops.

Cohesion

4. Wet the toothpick in the cup of water, then hold it very near—but not touching—one of the drops on the waxed paper. What happens to the drop? Try using the toothpick to drag a drop across the waxed paper. What happens when one drop meets another?

ACTION, REACTION, RESULTS

Water molecules are attracted to each other. Because of this, the drops are attracted to each other and to the water on the toothpick. This attractive force is called cohesion.

HEAT WAVE

When you leave certain metal objects out in the rain, a chemical reaction takes place. Rust is the product of that reaction.

Setup time: 25 minutes • **Observation time:** 5 minutes

MATERIALS

 glass jar with lid outdoor thermometer to fit in the jar

 I soap-free steel wool scouring pad

 vinegar  bowl

DIRECTIONS

1. Put the thermometer in the jar and close the lid. Wait 5 minutes, then note the temperature.

5 minutes

2. Pull the steel wool pad apart to loosen the fibers. Place it in the bowl and cover it with vinegar. Wait 5 minutes.

5 minutes

> **WORD FILE**
>
> **Oxidize:** To add oxygen to a substance.
>
> **Rust:** A reddish-colored coating of oxidized iron.

Chemical Reaction

3. Take the steel wool out of the vinegar and allow it to drain. Remove the thermometer from the jar. Wrap the steel wool around the bulb of the thermometer, put it back into the jar, and replace the lid.

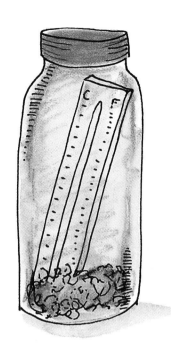

4. Wait 5 minutes, then note the temperature again.

5 minutes

ACTION, REACTION, RESULTS

The temperature rises after you put the steel wool into the jar. By soaking the steel wool in the vinegar you remove any coating. The iron in the steel begins to oxidize and produce rust. The process produces heat, which causes the temperature in the jar to rise.

SAY CHEESE

Mix lemon juice with milk and you'll create a gooey mess, that is, unless you heat it first.

Setup time: 30 minutes ● **Observation time:** 5 minutes

MATERIALS

 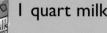 2 tablespoons lemon juice cup saucepan

 1 quart milk wooden spoon cheesecloth

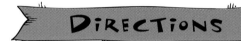 colander small bowl stove

DIRECTIONS

1. Pour 2 tablespoons of lemon juice into a cup.

2. With an adult helper, pour the milk into the saucepan and turn on the burner to medium-high. Stir slowly with a wooden spoon and watch for small bubbles to form.

3. Once the milk begins to boil, remove the pan from the stove. Stir in the lemon juice.

4. Return the saucepan to the stove and continue to stir on medium heat until lumps begin to form. Turn off the stove, remove the saucepan from the burner, and allow the mixture to cool for 5 minutes.

5 minutes

Protein Coagulation

5. Place the colander in the sink, line it with cheesecloth, and pour the mixture into it. The lumps, called curds, will collect in the bottom.

6. Once the liquid has drained away, put the curds into a small bowl and refrigerate. You might want to add a little salt before you eat this cheese.

ACTION, REACTION, RESULTS

Adding lemon juice, a mild acid, to warmed milk causes the protein in the milk to form lumps, or to coagulate. The end result is a homemade form of cottage cheese.

WORD FILE

Coagulate: To thicken.

Protein: Substance made up of hundreds or even thousands of simpler units linked together called amino acids. Amino acids contain carbon, hydrogen, oxygen, nitrogen, and sometimes sulfur.

MINING FOR IRON

Have you heard of people having muscles of steel?
Maybe it's because they get so much iron in their fruit juice.

Setup time: 15 minutes ● **Observation time:** 4½ hours

MATERIALS

 pint glass jar 4 tea bags water

 3 small glasses 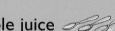 measuring cup

 pineapple juice, white grape juice, apple juice 3 plastic spoons

DIRECTIONS

1. Put all four tea bags into the jar and fill it to the top with warm water. Let the jar sit for 2 hours.

2 hours

2. Pour ¼ cup of tea solution into each of the three glasses.

3. Rinsing the measuring cup after each juice, pour ¼ cup of pineapple juice into the first glass, ¼ cup of white grape juice into the second glass, and ¼ cup of apple juice into the third glass.

4. Let the glasses sit for 30 minutes, then lift each glass and check to see if any dark particles have settled on the bottom.

30 minutes

2 hours

5. Let the glasses sit for another 2 hours, then check again for dark particles.

ACTION, REACTION, RESULTS

A chemical reaction takes place when chemicals in the tea come in contact with iron in the juice. Dark particles form and settle to the bottom of the glass. The pineapple juice contains a lot of iron so a lot of particles form quickly. It takes longer for particles to develop in the white grape juice. No particles develop in the apple juice because it does not contain iron.

> Iron is important in the human body for several reasons. Iron is what makes blood red and enables blood to carry oxygen. Iron also plays an important part in the liver in breaking down toxins.

CURRENTS OF COLOR

Which is heavier, warm water or cold water?
This experiment in density will help you find the answer.

Setup time: 15 minutes • **Observation time:** 10 minutes

MATERIALS

paper cup • pencil • glass quart jar

warm water • measuring cup

cold water • ice • food coloring

DIRECTIONS

1. Fill the glass jar nearly to the top with warm water.

2. Use the pencil to poke four holes around the bottom edge of the cup.

3. Fill the measuring cup with ½ cup of cold water. Stir in 5 drops of food coloring. Add two cubes of ice and stir.

4. Place the paper cup into the warm water in the jar. Quickly pour the cold water into the cup. What happens when the cold, colored water contacts the warm water?

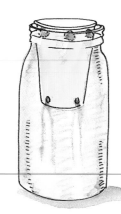

ACTION, REACTION, RESULTS

Density is the measure of the amount of matter that is in a given space. The molecules of the cold water are more numerous and closer to each other than the molecules in a similar amount of warm water, so cold water is heavier. It sinks to the bottom of the jar in colorful curls.

WATER BAG

Punch a hole in a bag full of water, and you'll get all wet—
unless the bag happens to be made from certain polymers.

Setup time: 5 minutes ● **Observation time:** 2 minutes

MATERIALS

 self-sealing plastic sandwich bag

 water  sharp pencil

DIRECTIONS

1. Fill the plastic bag with water and seal it.

2. Hold up the bag with one hand. Hold the pencil with the other hand, and in a quick, stabbing motion, stick it through one side of the bag and out the other. Does the bag leak?

ACTION, REACTION, RESULTS

Certain types of molecules form long chains called polymers. Some are natural and some are manufactured. Polyethylene is a type of plastic made from polymers and used to make plastic bags. Polyethylene has a unique quality: it shrinks when ripped or when a hole is poked in it. When you poke a hole in the bag with the pencil, the plastic seals around the pencil and doesn't leak.

OLDIE MOLDY

Some plants reproduce by seeds and some reproduce by spores.
The spores needed to grow your own mold are as close
by as a patch of house dust.

Setup time: 20 minutes ● **Observation time:** 4 days

MATERIALS

 3 pieces of bread   spray bottle of water

 3 self-sealing plastic sandwich bags

 stick-on labels   marker

DIRECTIONS

1. Mist three slices of bread with water until they are damp but not soaking wet.

2. Find a dusty spot—under a bed or in a closet—and wipe up some dust onto the bread. Slip the slice into a plastic bag and seal it. Label the bag and write down where you found the dust.

Spores

3. Repeat the steps with the second piece of bread, but get dust from a different spot. Do the same with the third slice.

4. Place all of the labeled bags in a warm, dark place. Check them daily but don't open the bags. On the fourth day, how does the bread look?

4 days

ACTION, REACTION, RESULTS

Tiny spores float through the air and spread over great distances. Most house dust contains mold spores. When the spores finally come in contact with a moist place where food is available, they grow. The bread picks up mold spores when you rub it in house dust. The damp bread provides an excellent environment for the molds to reproduce and grow.

WORD FILE

Fungi: Plural of fungus.

Mold: A kind of fungus.

Spore: A reproductive cell formed by certain plants such as ferns or fungi. The spores of fungi are often very tiny.

BAKED ICE CREAM

Insulation can keep things hot or cold. You can demonstrate how it works by baking a great ice cream treat in the oven.

Setup time: 30 minutes ● **Observation time:** 5 minutes

MATERIALS

 oven 2 egg whites 2 tablespoons sugar

 medium-sized glass bowl mixer 6 vanilla wafers

 cookie sheet spoon vanilla ice cream

DIRECTIONS

1. Preheat the oven to 250 degrees Fahrenheit.

2. In a clean, dry glass bowl, whip two egg whites with the mixer on high. Beat 2 minutes. Add 2 tablespoons sugar. Whip until the mixture makes stiff, glossy peaks.

3. Place the cookies on a cookie sheet. Spoon a walnut-sized mound of ice cream onto the center of each cookie.

> **A similar dessert made with cake, ice cream, and egg whites is called a "Baked Alaska."**

4. Coat each ice cream topped cookie with a thick layer of egg white mixture. Be sure to completely cover the ice cream and cookie. Bake them in the oven just until the egg white turns light brown, about 3 or 4 minutes. Remove from the oven and enjoy. Is the ice cream still cold?

ACTION, REACTION, RESULTS

Insulation prevents cold or heat from draining away. Layers of air within or between materials improve the efficiency of insulation. By whipping the egg whites you add air to the mixture. In the oven, the air bubbles prevent the heat from getting to the ice cream. When you eat the treat, the egg white mixture is warm, but the ice cream remains cold.

SINK OR FLOAT

Salt water is heavier than fresh (plain, unsalted) water.
An egg can help you to prove it.

Setup time: 10 minutes ● **Observation time:** 5 minutes

MATERIALS

 2 glasses — Salt — 5 tablespoons salt

2 raw eggs — water

DIRECTIONS

1. Fill the first glass halfway with water. Mix in 5 tablespoons of salt. Gently place an egg on the salt water. Does it float or sink?

2. Fill the second glass halfway with fresh water. Place an egg in the water. Does it float or sink?

ACTION, REACTION, RESULTS

Salt water is more dense than fresh water because of the salt content. There is more matter in a given amount of salt water than there is in a similar amount of fresh water. The egg easily floats in the salt water, but not in the fresh water, because the egg is less dense than the salt water and more dense than the fresh water.

Density

DOWN THE SPOUT

Amaze your friends by pouring water from a pitcher into a glass two feet away.

Setup time: 10 minutes • **Observation time:** 5 minutes

MATERIALS

 1-quart pitcher water food coloring

 3 feet of cloth string drinking glass

DIRECTIONS

1. Fill the pitcher halfway with water, add several drops of food coloring, and stir.

2. Soak the string for a moment in the water, then take it out and let it drain back into the pitcher.

3. Tie one end of the string to the handle of the pitcher. Set the glass on a flat surface 2 feet away.

4. With one hand, hold the pitcher about a foot high. With the other hand, hold the loose end of the wet string. Stretch the string tightly across the spout of the pitcher, and hold the loose end against the inside of the glass.

5. Slowly pour a trickle of colored water down the string and into the glass. Can you fill the glass without spilling?

ACTION, REACTION, RESULTS

Cohesion is the tendency of a material to stick to itself. As you pour the water from the pitcher, it is attracted to the water on the already wet string. Another force is at work here as well. The molecules of some substances are attracted to the molecules of other substances. This is called adhesion. In this experiment, the water is attracted to the string and tends to cling to it.

Cohesion and Adhesion

SLIP AND SLIDE

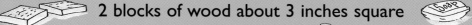

If it weren't for friction, it would be difficult to stay on your feet as you walk across the floor. Use this demonstration to learn more about this gripping force.

Setup time: 5 minutes • **Observation time:** 15 minutes

MATERIALS

 2 blocks of wood about 3 inches square   soap

2 flat metal jar lids   cooking oil

DIRECTIONS

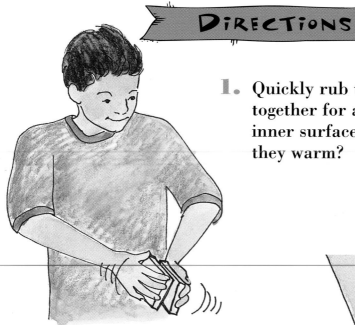

1. Quickly rub the two blocks of wood together for about a minute. Feel the inner surfaces of the wood blocks. Are they warm?

2. Coat the inner surfaces of the wood blocks with a layer of soap. Rub them together again for about a minute, then check. Are they warm? Were they easier to rub together this time?

3. Rub the flat surfaces of the two metal lids together for about a minute. Do they become warm? Do they make a noise?

4. Coat the flat surfaces of the lids with cooking oil, then rub them together again. Do they feel warm this time? Did they make as much noise as they rubbed together?

ACTION, REACTION, RESULTS

Most surfaces are rough. Even those that look smooth have tiny imperfections. When two surfaces are rubbed together, the imperfections catch on each other and create resistance, or friction. It takes energy to make the surfaces move across each other, and much of that energy is turned into heat. The soap and oil are lubricants. They coat the surfaces and make them slide past each other more easily. With less friction, less heat is generated.

Friction can be put to good use. The brake on a bicycle works by friction. When it's used, the brake presses against the turning wheel and creates friction that slows or stops the wheel. Lubricants are useful, too. They are used to coat moving parts in machines to prevent them from wearing out or getting too hot.

CRUNCH

At this moment air is pushing on you and everything around you. You usually don't notice it, but here's a way to see how powerful air can be.

Setup time: 15 minutes • **Observation time:** 1 hour

MATERIALS

 1-liter plastic soda bottle with cap

 warm water

 1 cup crushed ice

 funnel

DIRECTIONS

5 minutes

1. Fill the bottle with warm water and let it sit for 5 minutes.

2. Empty the bottle. Use the funnel to pour 1 cup of crushed ice into the bottle as quickly as possible, then tightly screw on the

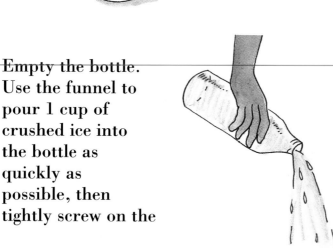

3. Shake the bottle, then place it where it can remain undisturbed for at least 1 hour. What happens?

1 hour

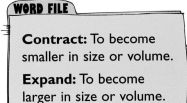

ACTION, REACTION, RESULTS

Molecules of air spread out when they are heated and move together when they are chilled. By warming the air in the bottle with warm water, you cause the air inside to expand. When you put in the ice, you chill the air and it contracts and lowers the pressure inside the bottle. The air pressure outside the bottle is greater, so eventually the sides of the bottle collapse.

WORD FILE

Contract: To become smaller in size or volume.

Expand: To become larger in size or volume.

LiGHTS OUT

Certain substances create strange chemical reactions when they combine. Some chemical reactions can be very useful.

Setup time: 15 minutes ● **Observation time:** 5 minutes

MATERiALS

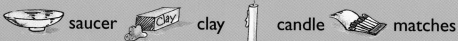 saucer clay candle matches

 drinking glass 2 tablespoons baking soda ¼ cup vinegar

cardboard tube from a roll of bathroom tissue

DiRECTiONS

1. Press a walnut-sized ball of clay into the center of the saucer. Stand up the candle in the center of the clay. Ask an adult to light the candle.

2. In the glass, mix 2 tablespoons of baking soda and ¼ cup of vinegar to create carbon dioxide gas.

3. Quickly, hold the cardboard tube near—but not touching—the candle flame. Tip the glass as if you were pouring the invisible carbon dioxide gas through the tube and over the candle like water. Be careful not to pour out any of the baking soda–vinegar mixture. What happens to the flame?

ACTiON, REACTiON, RESULTS

Carbon dioxide gas will not burn. Many fire extinguishers work by pumping foam over flames. The foam is a blanket of bubbles of carbon dioxide gas.

Fire uses oxygen in the air as fuel. By combining baking soda and vinegar, you begin a chemical reaction that produces carbon dioxide gas. Carbon dioxide gas is heavier than air. That is why you can pour it through the tube and over the candle flame. The gas replaces the air around the flame and extinguishes it.

54

PRESSURE POINT

As an ice skater glides across the ice, the pressure from the blades of the skates melts the ice beneath the blades. The skater actually glides on a thin layer of water.

Setup time: 10 minutes • **Observation time:** 1 hour

MATERIALS

 corked bottle ice cube

 3½-inch piece of strong, thin wire   2 heavy bolts

DIRECTIONS

1. Twist one end of the wire around the bolt. Twist the other end of the wire around the other bolt.

2. With the cork in the bottle, balance the ice cube on the top of the cork. Drape the wire over the center of the ice cube.

3. Put the bottle in the refrigerator and check it every 15 minutes until the wire is resting on the cork.

ACTION, REACTION, RESULTS

The pressure of the wire melts the ice directly underneath it. The wire moves down through the water, which re-freezes behind it. The wire will travel slowly through the ice cube all the way to the cork, but it won't cut the cube in two.

WORD FILE

Pressure: A pushing or squeezing force that works on a given area.

SWEET OR SALTY

Sugar and salt certainly have different tastes, but they look a lot alike. Here's a way to tell them apart without tasting them.

Setup time: 10 minutes • **Observation time:** 10 minutes

MATERIALS

 2 small saucepans

 1 teaspoon salt

 1 teaspoon sugar

 stove

DIRECTIONS

1. Mix up the teaspoons so you are not sure which is salt and which is sugar.

2. With an adult helper, place each saucepan on a burner on the stove. Put the contents of the first spoon in the first pan and the contents of the second spoon in the second pan.

3. Turn on both burners to medium heat and watch for a few minutes. Do any changes take place?

ACTION, REACTION, RESULTS

WORD FILE

Carbon: An element, which is a substance made up entirely of atoms of all the same kind.

Nothing happens to the salt. It remains white and grainy. The sugar turns brown and begins to melt. Heating sugar causes its molecules to separate into carbon, turning it brown, and hydrogen and oxygen in the form of water.

Identifying Sugar

HOMEGROWN GEMS

Things don't have to be alive to grow.
You can grow your own garden of gems in a jar.

Setup time: 15 minutes ● **Observation time:** 2 weeks

MATERIALS

 glass quart jar warm water alum (available in supermarkets)

spoon pencil 10 inches of nylon thread paper clip

DIRECTIONS

1. Fill the jar with warm water to within an inch of the top.

2. Stir in the alum until no more will dissolve.

3. Tie the string around the center of the pencil.

4. Tie a paper clip to the other end of the string. Lower the paper clip into the jar. Rest the pencil across the top of the jar. Turn the pencil to shorten the string until the paper clip hangs an inch from the bottom.

5. Place the jar in a warm, sunny place where it will be undisturbed. Check on the progress every day or two as your crystals grow.

ACTION, REACTION, RESULTS

The molecules that make up crystals form a definite structure. By stirring alum into the warm water you create a solution. As the water evaporates, the molecules realign and produce crystals that cling to the string and sides of the jar. The crystals continue to form until all of the solution has evaporated.

WORD FILE

Alum: A chemical salt used in pickling.

Evaporate: To convert to vapor or to pass off moisture.

Solution: One or more substances dissolved in another substance, usually liquid.

MAKING MAYONNAISE

Mayonnaise looks simple on a sandwich, but to make this special spread, you have to make oil and "water" mix.

Setup time: 15 minutes ● **Observation time:** 5 minutes

MATERIALS

 blender 1 cup tofu 3 tablespoons vinegar

½ cup olive oil   glass pint jar with lid

DIRECTIONS

1. In the blender at slow speed, combine tofu and 1 tablespoon of vinegar.

2. Adjust blender to medium and add olive oil very slowly, a drop at a time. Use about a third of the oil, then add a tablespoon of vinegar.

3. Continue to add oil very slowly until two thirds has been added, then add the final tablespoon of vinegar. Blend in the last of the oil.

Emulsion

4. Pour your mayonnaise into a jar and refrigerate. You might want to add a little salt before you use your mayonnaise on a sandwich.

ACTION, REACTION, RESULTS

Mayonnaise is a substance known as an emulsion. Usually oil and water (in this case, oil and vinegar) don't mix. In this experiment, you use an emulsifier, the tofu, to surround the droplets of oil and separate them from each other. The individual oil droplets are suspended in the vinegar.

WATER POWER

Create a water fountain in your kitchen sink and learn about water pressure at the same time.

Setup time: 15 minutes • **Observation time:** 5 minutes

MATERIALS

 ½-gallon paper milk carton large nail

 masking tape water

DIRECTIONS

1. With the nail, make three holes in one side of the milk carton in line from top to bottom. Make the first hole 1 inch from the bottom and make the second and third holes in line above it, each 1 inch apart.

2. Cover the holes with masking tape.

3. Place the carton in the sink under the tap. Fill it with water.

4. Remove the tape. The water will stream out. Which stream flows the farthest?

ACTION, REACTION, RESULTS

Water has weight, and the weight creates pressure. The water in the carton pushes down and out against the sides of the carton. Because of the weight of the water above it, the water pressure is highest at the bottom of the carton, and that stream sprays farther than the others.

A MATTER OF BALANCE

Even when you are sitting still, your muscles are constantly making tiny adjustments to keep you balanced. At the center of this balancing act is your center of gravity.

Setup time: 20 minutes ● **Observation time:** 10 minutes

MATERIALS

 1-inch-thick slice of raw potato pencil

 corked bottle 2 forks

DIRECTIONS

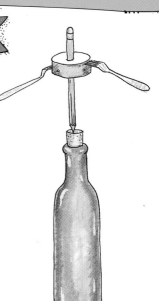

1. Place the corked bottle on a flat surface.

2. Try to balance the pencil on its point on the cork. Is it possible?

3. Push the pencil through the center of the potato slice.

4. Push the tines of the forks into the edge of the potato opposite each other.

5. Now try to balance the pencil on its point on the cork. If it doesn't balance, adjust the forks until it does.

ACTION, REACTION, RESULTS

All objects have a point of balance at which they are perfectly balanced and will not fall. This is called the center of gravity. At first, the pencil in this experiment cannot balance on its point. By adding the potato slice and forks you can adjust the setup until you find the proper center of gravity.

SECRET MESSAGE

You can surprise your friends by using this recipe for invisible ink.

Setup time: 15 minutes ● **Observation time:** 5 minutes

MATERIALS

1 lemon 　 juicer 　 small bowl

cotton swab 　 white paper 　 lamp

DIRECTIONS

1. Squeeze the juice from the lemon into a small bowl.

2. Dip the cotton swab into the lemon juice and use it to write an invisible message on a clean sheet of white paper. Allow the "ink" to dry.

3. Hold the paper very close to—but not touching—an exposed light bulb. Move the paper so that the entire message is exposed to the heat from the bulb. What happens?

ACTION, REACTION, RESULTS

The lemon juice contains carbon compounds. When exposed to heat, these compounds tend to turn brown or black. When heated with the light bulb, the invisible message turns dark and becomes readable.

HANGING AROUND

Can you pick up an ice cube with a string?
This surprising experiment will show you how.

Setup time: 5 minutes ● **Observation time:** 2 minutes

MATERIALS

 drinking glass water ice cube

 4-inch piece of string salt

DIRECTIONS

1. Fill the glass nearly to the top with water.

2. Float an ice cube in the water. Hold the string at one end and drape the other end across the ice cube.

3. Sprinkle a pinch of salt around the end of the string that is on the ice cube.

4. Count slowly to 10, then pull on the end of the string that you are holding to lift the ice cube out of the water.

ACTION, REACTION, RESULTS

Water freezes at 32 degrees Fahrenheit. Salt water freezes at a lower temperature than that. By sprinkling salt on the ice cube, you lower its melting point, causing it to melt slightly around the string. The fluid that flows under the string quickly turns to ice again, freezing the string in place.